"Everyone has an invisible

sign hanging from his or

her neck saying, 'Make

me feel important.'"

– Mary Kay Ash

The Manager's Motivation Handbook

How to Develop Passion and Positive Performance With Everyone On Your Team

SUSAN FEE

The
Manager's
Motivation
Handbook

The Walk the Talk Company
P.O. Box 210996
Bedford, TX 76095

Printed in the United States of America
13-digit ISBN: 978-1-885228-94-9

Credits

Copy Editor	Kathleen Green, Positively Proofed, Plano, TX
	info@PositivelyProofed.com
Design, art direction & production	Melissa Cabana, Back Porch Creative, Plano, TX
	info@BackPorchCreative.com

INTRODUCTION

It's Monday morning and your alarm goes off.
What motivates you to get up and go to work?

It's a classic question with a multitude of possible answers: money, satisfaction, responsibility, challenge, and security are just a few examples. Figuring out what motivates your staff will be key to your success as a manager. That's because employee motivation affects every aspect of your business, including hiring, training, productivity, marketing, retention, and profit.

But, of course, you want more than people merely *showing up* for work. How do you inspire them to care? Let's assume you can't hand out huge raises from an unlimited budget (even if you could, the effect would be short-lived).

You've probably already tried pep talks or threats, with varying results. Some people get it, but then you've got a handful of toxic employees who are one massive energy drain. No matter what you do, they won't budge. If you're not careful, their negative attitudes can infect the rest of your staff.

Inspiring leaders don't constantly push or pull employees to excel. Instead, they walk beside them, offering coaching and encouragement to achieve self-directed goals.

Here's the bottom line: It's not your job to motivate your staff but, rather, to create a culture in which they become self-motivated.

Where do you stand right now? Here's the litmus test: How well does your staff perform in your absence? If people slack off the minute you're not around, then it's a sign that you've been doing too much of the motivating work. This handbook will teach you how to re-direct your efforts for a much better payoff.

First, a few basic truths about motivation that you'll need to know before reading further:

+ **Motivation is individual.** Everyone is motivated by something, but it's different for each person. There's not a universal formula that you can apply to your whole staff. You'll have to get to know people on an individual basis to understand what makes them tick.

+ **Limitations exist.** Accept that there will be certain things you can't change. You may not control the budget, benefits, hours, or that certain undesirable tasks still need to get done. But, there's a lot you can do to build a workforce that's engaged, investing in relationships being the No. 1 thing.

+ **People have limitations.** Not all employees share a deep desire to reach their full potential. In fact, maintaining the status quo is the main motivation for some people. If that's the case, they may never fit into the work culture you're building, no matter how hard you try.

+ **False praise gets false results.** Pumping people full of praise in hopes of getting them excited has the opposite effect when they haven't earned the accolades through hard work, or they don't hold the same self-perception. External motivators may work short-term, but they're not a long-term solution because they're not sustainable.

+ **Inspiring leaders are inspired.** You're the main role model for motivation! What drives you to do better? Everything that you want from your staff, you'll need to demonstrate yourself. So, how are you doing, really?

Motivation is an inside job. It's *intrinsic*, meaning that it's a drive that comes from within an individual to fulfill a personal goal or desire. While the seed of motivation is planted internally, it's affected by external factors such as: environment, tasks, co-workers, communication, rewards, promotions, and feedback. In other words, *you can't motivate your employees, but you can influence what they're motivated to do.*

Creating a motivation-rich work culture is similar to planting a garden. For a seedling to thrive, it must have the right conditions. The soil must be tilled and weeded. The seed must receive the right amount of water, fertilizer, sunlight, and room to grow according to its individual needs.

But the work isn't over with the preparation and planting. It's just beginning! The garden needs constant tending, weeding, trimming, feeding, and sometimes even re-planting. Given the right conditions and attention, the seedling blossoms.

There are some gardeners, though, who don't care about conditions, only about how things appear on the surface. When a weed pops up, they pluck it off at the stem without ever digging up the roots. So, of course, the weed returns. Managers expecting to motivate staff with a quick-fix approach are making the same mistake.

The symptom is not the problem.

Low motivation is at the root of many employee performance problems, but if you don't take the time to dig deeper, you'll mislabel the symptoms as the problem. Lack of effort, absenteeism, employee dissatisfaction, tardiness, resisting new ideas, chronic complaining, missed deadlines, poor communication, and repeated mistakes are all signs that something's wrong – but these are only symptoms. They don't tell you *what* is wrong. If you treat the symptoms as the problem, you'll never resolve anything.

Why aren't your employees motivated? Get ready to dig.

It could be any number of reasons:

+ Low self-confidence.

+ Fear.

+ Lack of trust in you and/or the organization.

+ Poor training.

+ Dissatisfying work.

+ Unclear goals.

+ Feeling undervalued.

+ Little or no feedback.

+ Hiring or retaining the wrong people.

Once you get to the root of the issue, you can respond in a way that transforms problems into positive performance. Something motivated you to read this book; you probably already know what it feels like to be inspired to learn, grow and apply new skills. Now, it's time to learn how to do the same with your staff. So, turn the page, and let's get going!

"Leadership is the art of

getting someone else to

do what you want done

because he wants to do it!"

– Dwight Eisenhower

CONTENTS

Create a Positively Contagious Culture

Build a Common Purpose

Every work environment has a vibe. Either it's pulsing with positive energy, barely has a pulse, or is D.O.A. How would you describe your environment? Do people arrive eager to work or enter the doors like a slowly leaking tire? Whatever the vibe, it's contagious and you need to make sure the right thing is spreading. If you want a motivated staff, you have to create a culture that supports it.

Work culture describes the environment, how people interact, the way they go about their work, attitudes, and what's valued. Some characteristics are evident at first glance, and other aspects are slower to be revealed. Just talking about a positive work culture isn't enough. It takes effort and action to create it. When you promise a supportive culture, but employees experience the opposite, it's motivation that's seeping through the gap.

In a positive work culture, there's a common purpose. Tasks are achieved independently, but everyone works together interdependently to fulfill a larger goal. People understand how their contributions affect the big picture and why every individual matters. Ultimately, it's your job to help create a culture that nurtures, encourages and inspires self-motivated people to perform. Here are nine characteristics of a thriving and motivational work culture:

1. **Understanding your organization's history, values and goals.** Every employee needs to know and believe in the organization's story. Why does it exist? Who does it serve and how? Where is it going?

2. **Knowledge of competition.** Who is the competition and how does the organization differentiate itself? How does employee teamwork forge a common purpose to stand out from competitors?

3. **Clear job expectations.** Each person should have a thorough understanding of the skills and tasks required for the position, plus benchmarks to evaluate how well it's being done. There should be no discrepancy between a written job description and what an employee actually does on a daily basis.

4. **Understanding of individual roles.** While a detailed job description provides a micro-view, a role description offers a macro-view. How does each employee's role fit into the organization's mission? Employees need to know why what they do matters, who it impacts, and how their role adds value to the organization overall.

5. **Definition of success.** Employee success should be tied directly to the organization's purpose and be stated clearly:

To be successful here, you must _____. Examples of success measurements include customer satisfaction, cost-savings, quality care, and innovation. What *doesn't* work is when the organizational message for success doesn't match the reality of the culture.

6. **Autonomy.** A key to job satisfaction is having some amount of control. Give employees the "what" (purpose, goals, timelines) and the freedom to figure out the "how" (plan to achieve).

7. **Personalized incentives.** Cookie-cutter incentive plans don't work because people are motivated for different reasons. The only way to understand what drives an individual is by asking and developing personal relationships.

8. **Open communication.** A universal sign of respect is acknowledgement. When you talk to your staff and really listen, you show that you care. It's not enough to say that you have an open-door policy, because many employees will still feel intimidated. You need to go to their turf and strike up conversations.

9. **Trust and transparency.** Employees must believe you're trustworthy enough to deliver on the first eight characteristics. Trust is built over time based on consistent behavior. Every time you say one thing and do another, you're revealing the truth about your work culture.

Each of these factors deserves equal attention. Think of each one as a rope in a large net that's woven together to support your staff. Missing strands eventually weaken the net, leaving holes for people to fall through. Take a quick measure of your current culture with the pronoun test. Listen for whether employees describe the organization as "we" or "they." Using "we" suggests they feel part of a team while "they" suggests some level of disengagement.

At this point you may be thinking, "Why should I be putting forth all this effort for my employees when they're the ones lacking motivation?" Because it's the only part you can control. You can't wait for people to become motivated and then build a positive culture to reward them. It starts with the right environment (like soil) to produce the performance you want.

CONNECT AND COMMUNICATE

It's not uncommon today to spend more time with the people you work with than with your friends and family. That's why work relationships matter. If you love your job, but dislike the people, it's hard for you to be motivated and in turn motivate others. The biggest influence you have as a manager is communication with your staff. **First and foremost, you are a relationship manager.**

Personal relationships are at the heart of trust and loyalty. It's much easier to skimp on a job when you don't really know the person you're letting down. When the American Psychological Association asked people why they stayed at their jobs, 40 percent of the people polled said it was because of their manager. What would your staff say about you? It depends on how well you've connected.

First and foremost, you are a relationship manager.

Your management role requires you to maintain a delicate balance between professional and personal issues. While you certainly don't want to try to become close friends, you do want to be friendly. Here are seven examples of ways you can connect with your staff to build positive relationships:

Observe. Pay attention to the little details that people reveal. If they're biking to work, compliment their healthy habits. If someone displays pictures of family, pets or hobbies, show interest. If people are reading books or listening to music on breaks, inquire about their interests.

Ask. The easiest way to learn about people is to ask. Professionally, ask about progress on a project, obstacles, successes, new ideas, and goals. Learn what they find motivating and meaningful about work. On a personal level, periodically check in with people and ask how they're doing.

Recall. Remember details and follow up. If you've learned someone was training for a marathon or had a child performing in a concert, be sure to ask how the event went, which communicates you were really listening.

Spread positive gossip. When you hear a customer or co-worker complimenting an employee, share the good news. Let the person know you heard others speaking highly of him or her.

Give feedback. Offer frequent updates on how well employees are completing job tasks and fulfilling their role on your team. Keep everyone in the loop on the organization's goals and direction.

Praise the process. The most helpful feedback highlights the process, not outcome. Be specific rather than merely saying, "Good job!" Discuss how the end result was achieved, such as decisions, asking the right questions, teamwork, or ingenuity. This type of feedback tells the employee what to specifically repeat next time, increasing both confidence and autonomy.

Say "thanks." Two words go a long way in building relationships: *Thank you.* Acknowledging people's efforts and accomplishments reminds them that what they do *really* matters.

> *Persuasion is lubricated by identifying a bond of commonality; taking time to establish one is not a detour but an essential step.*
>
> – DANIEL GOLEMAN

Establishing a good rapport with your staff is essential to creating a positive bond. Rapport can be defined as having a close and harmonious relationship, feeling in sync, relating well, and having a mutual understanding. The stronger your rapport, the more your staff will find that you are relatable, likable and inspiring.

Here are the three most important characteristics of relatable leaders:

1. **Embrace mistakes.** Everyone makes mistakes, but it's how you respond to them that reveals your true character. When you swiftly admit them, accept accountability and communicate the lessons you learned, you inspire others to do the same.

2. **Balance strength and vulnerability.** Leaders need to display confidence and decision-making, but – at the same time – sensitivity. You're not a leader if no one agrees to follow, and that's exactly what will happen if you lack empathy for the personal side of business.

3. **Share your story.** It's impossible to relate to someone if you don't know anything about the person. Be willing to share part of your personal story, when appropriate. What's your career story? What or who inspires you? What are your hobbies and passions? What lessons have you learned from your mistakes? What challenges have you overcome and how? These stories help to humanize you beyond the "boss" title and give people reasons to connect.

Remember, your work culture ultimately reflects what's valued. When you focus on building positive relationships through open communication, you show that you value *people*. This is the type of long-term investment that money can't buy. You're laying the groundwork for a passionate, loyal workforce.

Control What You Control

THE TRUTH ABOUT MOTIVATION

As a manager, what are you really managing? The obvious answer is "people," but if you said that, you'd be wrong. You can't manage anything you can't control. In fact, the more you try to control people, the more they resist. So, let's start with a reality check about what's really within your control.

Within your control	Outside of your control
Communication	Competitor decisions
Culture	Outside motivators
Expectations	Business circumstances
Systems	Time
Environment	Economy
Some resources	Customer expectations
Some hiring/training	Marketplace changes
Personal motivation	Technology advancements

The key to being an effective manager is to focus only on the things you can control and adapt to the rest. You might have noticed that "outside motivators" is on the list of things you can't control. But wait a minute – isn't this handbook supposed to teach you how to motivate your staff?

Yes, by focusing on the right things on the job that you can positively influence and control.

> *If you hire people just because they can do a job, they'll work for your money. But if you hire people who believe what you believe, they work for you in blood, sweat, and tears.*
> — SIMON SINEK

There was a time when people had little choice in the work they did. You took what was available near your home, mostly repetitive, labor-intensive or assembly-line positions. People were grateful just to have a job. The industrial age depended on worker compliance. There was no talk of career advancement, flextime or work/life balance.

Work has changed significantly since then, but many assumptions about what motivates employees has not. It turns out, people are not like horses and don't respond well over time to carrots or whips. Money, fear, threats, and coercion are examples of extrinsic (external) motivators. They're outside factors used to influence a person's behavior, such as encouraging a student to earn better grades by paying for every "A." Take away the incentive and the grades drop. The mindset becomes: I'll do it only if you pay me. Once you start offering incentives, you can never go back.

Extrinsic motivation can produce results in some short-term cases, but in the long run, it's not sustainable. The responsibility falls on your shoulders to come up with the most enticing incentive just to get people to do a job. Once it's done, you have to rev them up all over again. It's exhausting – and expensive.

A better way to go is to focus on intrinsic (internal) motivation, which is what drives a person internally to achieve – regardless of outside forces. Remember, everyone is motivated to achieve something, although it may not be the same thing you want or need.

Abraham Maslow was one of the first psychologists who realized that people have different motivations based on their personal needs. He developed what's now known as Maslow's Hierarchy of Needs.

His theory suggested that our actions are motivated to meet certain basic needs first before we can advance to higher ones. Here's how it looks:

Maslow's Hierarchy of Needs

According to Maslow, if someone is solely concerned about earning enough money to pay the rent (physiological), that person isn't currently concerned about finding the most meaningful work (self-actualization). As a manager, you can increase work performance by understanding how to help people satisfy their intrinsic needs with an individualized approach. Here's how it might look:

Physiological

- Create an accommodating and comfortable work environment.

- Pay a competitive salary.

- Provide opportunities for people to earn more – if they choose – such as overtime, increased responsibilities, or promotion.

Safety

- Have clear rules and procedures in place and apply them fairly.

- Communicate often and remain available.

- Build trust by delivering on your word and behaving consistently.

Belonging

- Encourage group work and foster team-building.

- Give employees opportunities to learn by working with others.

- Highlight work in relation to others, the organization's purpose, and customer connection.

+ Communicate on a regular basis.

+ Connect employees who have similar interests.

Self-esteem

+ Regularly give positive feedback and praise the process of achievements.

+ Acknowledge performance results and say, "Thank you."

+ Allow for advancement opportunities into high-profile positions that highlight strengths.

+ Ask for opinions and involve people in planning and problem-solving.

Self-actualization

+ Allow autonomy.

+ Give the freedom to be creative.

+ Provide opportunities for more challenging work.

+ Facilitate problem-solving without immediately giving answers or directives.

+ Support personal and professional growth through training.

Remember, *control what you control and adapt to the rest.* You won't be able to meet every employee's needs. Do what you can and let go of the rest. Rather than focus on the limitations of your role or current circumstances, it's better to build awareness of what works and what you *can* do. And there are many "can do" opportunities for every manager.

Creative Ways to Recognize Employees

One factor that's always within your control is showing employees that you care. When you invest time in building relationships by recognizing employee efforts, you can spark renewed inspiration. Here are 20 low-cost, creative ways to recognize employees, which work quite effectively:

1. Encourage feedback from external and internal customers. Publicly post praise.

2. Remind staff how their work matters to customers, and encourage some level of customer interaction for everyone.

3. Call an employee into your office just to say "thank you" without discussing any other issue.

4. Write a thank-you card or email.

5. Send a note of congratulations to the employee's spouse/ family for something a family member achieved, such as graduation.

6. Create an employee newsletter to share updates and recognition.

7. Post a bulletin board for employees to share news, hobbies, and recognition.

8. Celebrate birthdays, anniversaries, and special achievements.

9. Create a change of pace by giving employees a chance to work on new projects or learn different skills.

10. Delegate worthy projects, not just menial tasks, to increase feelings of trust and confidence.

11. Create light-hearted awards that recognize something unique about each person, such as "Best Screen-Saver," or "Best Joke Teller," and present at a team meeting.

12. Pass on helpful articles that could benefit employees, attaching a note that says, "Saw this and thought of you."

13. Learn about their hobbies, families, children, pets, etc., showing interest in what matters most to people.

14. Ask an employee who is proficient in a certain area to train others or make a presentation at a staff meeting.

15. Book a community speaker to talk about subjects of interest to employees, such as personal finance, stress management, or improving relationships.

16. Help build skills with a training library filled with resources that employees can check out.

17. Allow employees to attend seminars, and ask them to make a presentation to others sharing what they learned.

18. Have one of your top performers mentor a new co-worker.

19. Invite current team members to be a part of the selection process for new team members.

20. Join in and help an employee who is under pressure. Ask what can be done and help complete the task side-by-side.

Personal Reflection

What's the most encouraging way a boss recognized your efforts? How did it affect your level of motivation?

"Expending energy trying to motivate people is largely a waste of time. If you have the right people on the bus, they will be self-motivated. The real question then becomes: How do you manage in such a way as not to de-motivate people?"

– Jim Collins

Getting Rid of De-Motivators

80/20 Rule

The Pareto Principle, also known as the 80/20 Rule, was developed in 1906 by an Italian economist who discovered that 80 percent of the land was owned by 20 percent of the population. The 80/20 rule is applicable in a number of situations: 20 percent of your customers produce 80 percent of your business, 20 percent of your time produces 80 percent of your results, 20 percent of your clothes represent what you wear 80 percent of the time, etc. The concept can be extremely helpful if you understand what inputs produce the highest desired outputs.

As a manager, the same rule holds true for people: A small percentage of your staff causes a disproportionate number of headaches. How much time and energy are you wasting trying to "fix" unfixable situations? And how much more efficient could you be by spending that time invested in the percentage of employees who complete the bulk of the work?

The goal, of course, is to help people be successful through appropriate coaching and opportunities. But sometimes the best way to help people be successful is to quit trying to fit them into an organization or job where they don't belong. Keeping these employees around acts as a de-motivator to high producers by creating a toxic work environment. It's important to evaluate the people on your current team to assess where to put your energy to increase maximum performance. Think in terms of three categories: dynamic, dependable and destructive.

DYNAMIC, DEPENDABLE OR DESTRUCTIVE?

When it comes to assessing levels of motivation, you'll find employees fall into one of three categories. First, you have the dynamic crowd. They consistently work hard, solve problems and are fully accountable. They often get overlooked because they don't cause problems, but that's a big mistake. Ignore these employees too long and they'll leave for better opportunities or backslide into average performers.

Workers who are dependable represent the core of your staff. They have a ton of potential but seem to be satisfied with average results. However, their lack of motivation may simply be a reaction to a negative work culture or poor communication. With a few adjustments, they can turn into dynamic and highly motivated performers.

A combination of the first two groups comprises the majority of your staff. Most of your energy should be poured into these people for the highest return on your investment of time. The remaining few will fall into the destructive category. These are the employees who are unable or refuse to meet performance standards no matter how hard you try to coach them or pump them up. This is that small group of toxic employees that can cause big problems as they drag you and everybody else down with them.

Let's take a closer look at how to identify the people in each category and how to respond. Start by grabbing a pad of paper and evaluating your team. Also, you'll need to honestly assess where you've been spending most of your time.

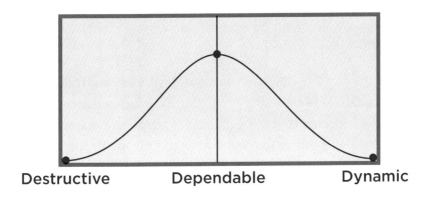

Destructive   **Dependable**   **Dynamic**

Dynamic Employees

Dynamic employees are your top-tier and best performers. They're self-motivated and have achieved a high level of autonomy, meaning they don't want or need to be micro-managed. But it's precisely because they know what they need to do and do it well without any prompting that they're easy to ignore. Don't confuse this efficiency as a sign that you can put them on autopilot.

Instead, these folks need and crave sincere recognition. Let them know that you appreciate their efforts and how important they are to you and your team. Remove any obstacles that prevent them from excelling even further. Consult with them about improving systems, procedures, timing, and communication.

Sometimes they're given the *wrong* attention by being asked to pick up the slack for less reliable co-workers. It can be highly de-motivating to these employees to be expected to do double the work just because they can and will. Soon they learn that it doesn't pay to work hard because all it gets them is more of other people's work. That's not to say dynamic employees aren't motivated by hard work – but it should be interesting and challenging. They're seeking to grow and master skills on projects that engage their strengths.

One of the main reasons dynamic employees are motivated to work so hard is because they've found meaning in their work and feel connected to the organization's purpose. Because they believe in the organization and you as their manager, they care. They know the "why" behind their work and that it matters. Center your communication around this idea by always keeping them in the loop with organizational goals, direction, and customer needs.

Dynamic Employees Need:

- ✦ Recognition
- ✦ Obstacles removed
- ✦ Challenging projects
- ✦ Constant connection to the organization's purpose

Dependable Employees

The majority of your staff falls into the category of dependable employees. They're "steady eddies" on the brink of becoming top performers but may feel held back by one or more issues, leaving them stuck in the middle ground of maintaining the status quo. They're not *bad* performers – they're just not motivated to be dynamic performers. Occasional performance problems may pop up, but nothing major. After you solve the issue, it's tempting to let this crew keep humming along at average.

So what's holding these employees back? It's your task to find out. There's a chance they'll be forthcoming and will tell you what they're lacking in order to move to a higher level. More than likely, though, their stagnation will show up in the form of symptoms like missed deadlines, incomplete work, complaining, and unnecessary mistakes. But, if you only spend time on the symptoms, you'll never get to the root of the problem.

Digging into the problem suggests these possibilities to explore: whether the employee *can* or *can't* perform and if the person *will* or *won't* perform. The ultimate combination is that employees *can* and *will* be high performers. But, dependable employees can be found in one of three remaining possibilities.

+ *Can/won't.* This person is able to do the job more effectively but is resistant. Possible reasons are a lack of trust, unclear goals, fear, low self-confidence, not wanting more work, or an unsupportive work culture.

+ *Can't/will.* This person is highly motivated and enthusiastic but lacks the training, skills, support, time, or tools to do the job.

◆ *Can't/won't.* This person may not be fully equipped for the position and is not motivated to do what's necessary to be successful. This could be due to not accepting change, fear, low self-confidence, or poor job placement.

None of these combinations make for an energized or fully productive employee. It's going to take some face-to-face time to find out what's behind each of your employee's symptoms. Once you do, mutually form an action plan to address the underlying issues. Avoid becoming the problem solver by providing all of the specific answers. This is definitely not where you want to focus your energy! Doing so undermines employee self-confidence and buy-in. Instead, be a facilitator of solutions. Finally, personally coach or consider a mentor to guide the employee through motivational challenges.

Dependable Employees Need:

◆ Attention paid to whether they can, can't, will, or won't

◆ Open-ended questions to help uncover the real problems

◆ Mutual problem-solving

◆ Coaching and/or mentoring

Destructive Employees

These toxic employees are the few who compromise your team's overall performance and can suck up most of your time if you're not careful. Destructive employees are morale-killers and act as de-motivators to the rest of your team. Whatever work they don't complete spills over to the rest of the staff, whose resentment is slowly brewing.

It may seem as though destructive employees aren't motivated.

The opposite may be true. It's just that they're motivated to do something other than what you need. They could have fallen into this category for a variety of reasons:

✦ Fear of change = motivated to maintain status quo

✦ Low confidence = motivated to protect exposure of weaknesses

✦ Boredom = motivated to find a new job

✦ Disillusionment = motivated to find an organization they believe in

✦ Entitlement = motivated by misguided expectations

Whatever landed employees in this category, there's no sense getting angry with them or assuming failure on your part. This is just what a bad fit looks like. All of the reasons listed are certainly coachable, but only if the employee wants to change. If you've created a positive culture, clearly communicated job expectations and roles, and provided consistent feedback regarding gaps between expectations and performance, then you've done all you can.

Destructive employees are revealing their true motivations through their behaviors. The smartest thing you can do is to believe their "what-you-see-is-what-you-get" performance sooner rather than later. If they choose not to change, they've fired themselves. The upside is that they're released to find something that better suits their strengths and interests.

Destructive Employees Need:

✦ Consistent feedback

✦ Frequent performance reviews

✦ Action plan to reach compliance

✦ Timeline to change or leave

Where Does Your Time Go?

✦ Which employees receive most of your attention?

✦ What issues receive most of your attention?

✦ How can you redistribute your time for a better return?

You don't always get to choose your staff – you inherit some people (and problems). But, when you have the chance, it's always the goal to hire the right people from the start. The best people will have more than just the skills for the job. Now you know how important it is that they fit into the organizational culture *and* believe in its mission. Here are examples of interview questions to help you find the best match:

Interview Questions: Cultural Fit

✦ Describe the work environment where you're the most productive and satisfied.

✦ What are the qualities of the best boss/organization that you've worked for or hope to work for?

✦ Do you prefer working alone or as part of a team? If it's a combination, in what percentages?

- Talk about a decision that you made that was based primarily on customer needs or input.

- Why do you believe you're a good fit for this organization?

- Suppose you overheard a team member giving incorrect information to a customer. What would you do in this situation?

- How would you deal with a new employee joining your team?

Interview Questions: Motivation

- Give an example of a challenging problem that you solved on your own.

- Give an example of a time when you felt extremely proud of an achievement. What part made you feel proud?

- What's your definition of career success?

- What career and personal goals have you set for yourself?

- What role does your manager play in your motivation at work?

- Imagine you are the boss. What would you do to make the workplace more motivating for your employees?

- What are the characteristics of an ideal working environment for you?

Strength-Building

RECOGNIZING TALENTS

Think back to your school days. What subjects were you excited to learn about and which classes did you dread? Maybe school itself was a bore, either because you found nothing about it interesting or it was so challenging that you gave up.

Most likely, the subjects you liked came easily to you. Even if they were hard, you liked the challenge. Therefore, you did better in those subjects than those you just didn't get. You probably weren't too motivated to spend time studying material you hated. Plus, you weren't that great at learning those subjects, so who wants to spend time doing something that feels like failure? Whatever did interest you – whether in or out of school – you were motivated to spend hours learning.

The same lessons in motivation extend to the workplace. Everybody naturally has areas where they excel. Because they can grasp the material or task easier than others, they tend to spend more time practicing, and therefore improving. But if you force people to go against their natural grain, you'll get resistance and poor performance.

When employees have the opportunity to do what they do best every day, they're naturally engaged, self-motivated, and have a positive impact on the work culture. Makes sense, right? It's more enjoyable to do what you're good at than spend most of your day struggling to do things that you're not.

When an employee's strengths are matched with the right job, performance skyrockets because people are doing what they do best.

Personal strengths are natural talents that have been cultivated and refined so that they can be applied consistently. **When an employee's strengths are matched with the right job, performance skyrockets because people are doing what they do best.**

Some people are aware of their strengths, but many are not. Since they're based on talents that come easily, people often don't appreciate the fact that their talents are unique. They assume everybody else can do it, too. Sometimes a person is a late bloomer, having never been exposed to his areas of potential interest or having never received the feedback or training necessary to perfect skills.

So your staff will come to you in various stages of strengths: fully aware, scratching the surface, or a diamond in the rough. As a manager, a large part of your success will be due to matching people's jobs to their talents and coaching them to develop strengths. Get this right and you'll have a driven, self-motivated staff.

Talent Quest

Talents can be described as naturally recurring patterns of thoughts, feelings or behaviors that have been present since childhood. Signs that point to your talents include areas of rapid learning and natural reactions. To help people recognize their talents, here are questions you can ask current employees and potential new hires:

- ✦ What activities can you pick up quickly after being shown just a few times?

- ✦ What activities have you taught yourself how to do out of curiosity?

- ✦ What activities are easy enough for you to skip steps or improvise because you can "see" or understand where it's going?

- ✦ What activities absorb your attention to the point of losing track of time?

- ✦ What activities do you find energizing?

- ✦ What seems to come easily to you but not always to others?

- ✦ What have others consistently told you that you're good at doing?

- ✦ Describe a project that you found deeply satisfying.

If these questions don't spark a theme, ask the employee to recall his childhood interests. Adulthood can sometimes quash natural childhood instincts that need to be rediscovered. How did he spend his free time? What made him different from other kids? How did he decorate his bedroom – with artwork, posters, collections, or trophies? All of these answers will reveal clues of innate interests and talents.

Red Light, Green Light

Another way to learn about talents is to pay attention to daily activities and energy levels. Give employees a self-awareness assignment. For one week at random daily intervals (up to eight times per day), have them write down four things:

1. Task they're doing

2. Level of energy and overall positive feelings on a scale of 1-10, with 10 being the highest

3. Whether other people were present or if done alone

4. Environment/setting

At the end of the week, spend time helping them uncover patterns and commonalities of the types of activities they ranked highest. (Note: Activities take effort and are different from time spent relaxing. So reading is an activity, but sleeping or watching TV doesn't count.) Create two lists, one titled "red" and the other "green."

Red list activities are the ones ranked low interest or were just "okay." Most likely, they were associated with dread, avoidance or procrastination. Green list activities are the ones ranked high and were enjoyable. They produced feelings of inspiration and desire to grow. Employees may need to keep trying different activities or applications in order to discover what really moves them. Sometimes it's a matter of mixing and matching talents with different parts, settings and people.

The nature of any business is that some of the work is unpleasant or boring. Realistically, you can't eliminate everyone's red list activities. But, if people can spend at least 80 percent of the day doing things they enjoy and are good at doing, they're bound to work much harder.

Examples of Talents

Remember, talents are just natural inclinations that show up in recurring patterns of how we think, feel and behave. They can be used in a number of ways. You will often have to help people make the leap from what they loved doing as a kid and how that can be applied at work. Here are some examples of talents:

- ◆ Communicating

- ◆ Organizing

- ◆ Socializing

- ◆ Analyzing

- ◆ Empathy

- ◆ Discipline

- ◆ Creativity

- ◆ Exploring

- ◆ Achievement

- ◆ Learning

- ◆ Ethics

- ◆ Curiosity

- ◆ Adaptability

As you can see, these attributes have multiple applications. When talents are applied in the right work setting, employees have the ability to reach what's known as a state of "flow." The term describes a level of concentration where a person is using his talents to reach a clearly stated goal that's achievable, but one that will take effort. If the task is too easy to achieve, you can make it harder, and if it is unattainable, you can increase skill training.

Athletes describe this state as "being in the zone" or the exhilarating "high" after working hard to achieve a goal. Anyone using his talents fully can experience it: a programmer cracking a difficult code, a salesperson closing a big deal, a customer service rep resolving a complicated issue, or a healthcare provider saving a life. What's the best part of operating in flow? The person is *self-motivated.*

7 Elements of Flow

1. Complete absorption in an activity.

2. Mentally energized, even if physically tired.

3. Inner clarity – clear on what needs to be done and doing it.

4. Knowing the task is achievable, even if difficult.

5. Inner calmness – no concerns about self.

6. Timelessness – hours seem to pass by in minutes.

7. Intrinsic motivation.

DEVELOPING STRENGTHS

It takes more than raw talent to be successful. If you've helped your employees recognize their talents, that's half the battle. But here's where your real work begins – developing those talents into strengths that translate into high performance. There are three things you'll need to add to talent to develop it into a reliable strength: knowledge, skills and managing weakness.

1) Knowledge

There are two types of knowledge to acquire: factual and experiential. Another way of putting it is, you need both book smarts and street smarts to be successful. One type of knowledge without the other leads to failure. Assess your staff's factual knowledge. Do they understand your industry, products, services, systems, and language? This type of knowledge doesn't guarantee success, but without it, employees will flounder.

With the foundation of factual knowledge in place, employees are ready for the "real world." These are the real-life experiences that give people the chance to apply what they've learned and then adapt in real time. This is where you turn over the reins and allow employees to figure things out for themselves. Remember, you're building on their talents and experiences, so they're motivated to learn.

Sometimes you'll have an employee who has a ton of real-life experience but no official training. These employees may seem like a bit of a wildcard but – with the proper support – can turn into top performers.

2) Skills

For strengths to be reliable and predictable, they need to be built around a framework of skills. When talents are taken for granted, people don't recognize the specific skills they use to achieve a goal. But if you break down their process, there's usually a repeated step-by-step plan.

By providing feedback on the process of *how* someone completes a task, you'll highlight the skills necessary. To do this, be prepared for the person to respond with an agitated, "I don't know – I just do it." Don't let this deter you. Provide your observations and encourage them to slow down and think out loud about their internal process. This will expose steps they take and if any skills are missing that you need to teach. By highlighting the process, you give them a success plan to replicate every time.

3) Manage Weaknesses

One of the reasons people get distracted from recognizing their strengths is because they've grown up with the belief that it's best to concentrate on improving "weaknesses." So if you're excellent in analysis but not so great at public speaking, it's often suggested that it's better to spend your time improving your presentation skills. But, the reality is, you may never be outstanding at public speaking if it's not your talent, no matter how hard you try. But you can definitely improve. On the other hand, if you love analysis, pick it up quickly, and would be energized by learning more, then attending a workshop on improving analytical skills would give you the knowledge to develop your strength.

Every work performance review includes "areas of opportunity." That's code for: Here's what you don't do very well. Most likely, these are weaknesses. Remember the 80/20 Rule. If you spend

80 percent of your time coaching employees on the 20 percent they don't do well (weaknesses), you're wasting everyone's time.

> *My main job was developing talent. I was a gardener providing water and other nourishment to our top 750 people. Of course, I had to pull out some weeds, too.*
> — JACK WELCH

Weaknesses are not necessarily liabilities. If they're recurring patterns, think of these characteristics as a misplaced talent. The true areas of growth are strengths because they're based on innate talents where there are endless opportunities (and motivation) to learn.

This doesn't mean you should totally ignore weaknesses. If they distract an employee from realizing strengths, offer coaching to minimize them. But don't expect people to excel in areas that are not strengths. Put most of your energy into helping people improve their strengths, and you will discover that many of their "weaknesses" will dissipate.

REVIEW AND CLOSING THOUGHTS

We've covered a lot of material about how to motivate your staff. You're now equipped with what it takes to develop passion and positive performance with everyone on your team. It's up to you to take the next step – *applying* what you've learned in this book. First, let's summarize the main points. Here are the 10 most important ideas to remember about employee motivation:

1. **Relationships matter.** Your personal connection with employees is the No. 1 factor you control. Building strong relationships is the core of building a positive work culture and being able to learn what motivates each individual. People will care when they know you care about them.

2. **Everyone is motivated.** Laziness is a myth. Everyone is motivated to achieve something, although it may not always be what you want or need.

3. **Motivation is personal.** You're not responsible for motivating your staff. Rather, it's your job to create the environment in which they can become self-motivated.

4. **Motivation is individual.** People are different and, therefore, what motivates each person is unique. There is no one-size-fits-all incentive plan that will work for everyone. You'll need an individualized approach.

5. **Make it meaningful.** Employees need to know why what they do matters, who it serves, and how their efforts add value to the organization.

6. **Carrots and whips don't work long-term.** Threatening, begging or cajoling employees to perform isn't effective or sustainable. Inspiring self-motivated employees means tapping into their internal motivators.

7. **Focus on controllable factors.** You don't have control over everything and you can't meet every employee need. Don't waste time worrying about what you can't do. Take action on those things within your control and adapt to the rest.

8. **Invest in the right people.** The majority of your staff wants to be there and is willing to work hard, given the right support. Helping dynamic and dependable employees develop their talents will lead to bigger payoffs than spending a disproportionate amount of time with destructive employees.

9. **Focus on strengths.** Put a high percentage of your energy on helping people enhance their strengths and you'll discover that many of their "weaknesses" will dissipate.

10. **Lead by example.** To inspire others, be inspired! Learn what motivates you, examine your personal strengths, invest in knowledge and skill training, and share your success stories. Positive energy is contagious.

Finally, a closing thought:

> *If your actions inspire others to dream more, learn more, do more and become more, you are a leader.*
> — JOHN QUINCY ADAMS

MOTIVATION BEST PRACTICES

Here's your opportunity to keep a running log of Motivation "Best Practices" that you have observed or discovered through your own experiences.

_____

_____

_____

_____

_____

_____

_____

_____

_____

_____

_____

_____

_____

_____

_____

_____

_____

_____

_____

_____

_____

_____

_____

_____

_____

_____

_____

_____

_____

_____

_____

_____

_____

_____

_____

_____

_____

_____

_____

_____

_____

_____

_____

_____

_____

_____

Be sure to motivate and help others by sharing these positive examples with your colleagues.

About the Author

Susan Fee is a clinical counselor, trainer, keynote speaker, coach, and human resource development professional. Known for her engaging and enlightening style, she helps individuals and clients dig deep to find their own source of inspiration. Her audiences span multiple industries, including health care, technology, finance, and education.

Learn more about Susan Fee's professional services and resources by visiting her website at www.**SusanFee**.com

About the Publisher

The Walk the Talk Company

Since 1977, our goal at Walk the Talk has been both simple and straightforward: to provide you and your organization with high-impact resources for your personal and professional success.

We believe in developing capable leaders, building strong communities, and helping people stay inspired and motivated to reach new levels of skills and confidence. When you purchase from us and share our resources, you not only support small business, you help us on our mission to make the world a more positive place.

Each member of the walkthetalk.com team appreciates the confidence you have placed in us, and we look forward to serving you and your organization in the future.

To learn more about us, visit **walkthetalk.com.**

How to Order this Book

The Manager's Motivation Handbook

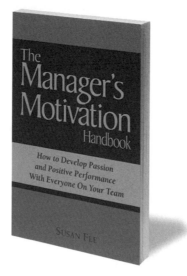

$10.95

To order additional copies of this powerful handbook,
visit **www.walkthetalk.com** or call us at 888.822.9255.
It would be our pleasure to help you with your ordering needs.

For quantity discounts, please email us at
info@walkthetalk.com or call **888.822.9255.**

Other Recommended Management Development Resources

 *The Manager's Communication Handbook* –
This powerful handbook will allow you to connect with employees and create the understanding, support and acceptance critical to your success. It will introduce you to the four key dimensions of communication and teach you how to eliminate communication barriers. **$10.95**

 *The Manager's Coaching Handbook* – A must-have handbook for leaders at all levels. This cut-to-the-chase resource provides managers, supervisors, and team leaders with simple, easy-to-follow guidelines for positively affecting employee performance. Within the pages, you'll find practical strategies for dealing with superior performers, those with performance problems, and everyone in between. **$10.95**

 *Listen Up, Leader* – Be the type of leader everyone will follow! This best-selling leadership book provides powerful insight into what employees want and need from their managers, supervisors, and team leaders. It pinpoints the behaviors and attributes necessary to be the kind of leader that employees will follow … to higher levels of success. **$10.95**

To learn more about our hundreds of resources designed to help managers become more effective and respected leaders, visit **www.walkthetalk.com**

Resources for Personal and Professional Success